EASY PIANO

2nd EDITION

# THE HALLOWEEN Songbook

ISBN 978-0-7935-6948-9

HAL•LEONARD®
CORPORATION
7777 W. BLUEMOUND RD. P.O. BOX 13819 MILWAUKEE, WI 53213

Visit Hal Leonard Online at
**www.halleonard.com**

# CONTENTS

# ADDAMS FAMILY THEME
## Theme from the TV Show and Movie

Music and Lyrics by
VIC MIZZY

creep - y and they're kook - y, mys - te - ri - ous and spook - y. They're
house is a mu - se - um where peo - ple come to see 'em. They

al - to - geth - er ook - y, the Ad - dams Fam - i - ly. The
real - ly are a scree - um, the

# CASPER THE FRIENDLY GHOST

**from the Paramount Cartoon**

Words by MACK DAVID
Music by JERRY LIVINGSTON

Lyrics:
Cas - per the friend - ly ghost, the friend - li - est ghost you know. Though grown - ups might look at him with fright, the chil - dren all love him so.

Cas - per the friend - ly ghost, he could - n't be bad or

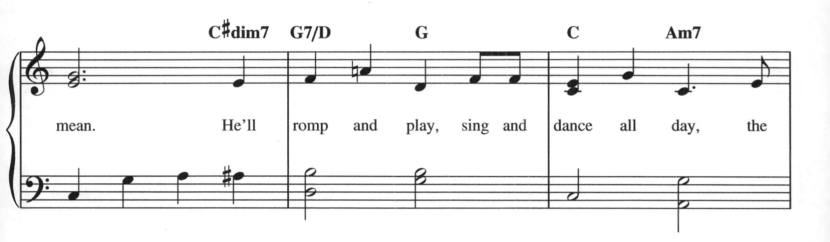

mean. He'll romp and play, sing and dance all day, the

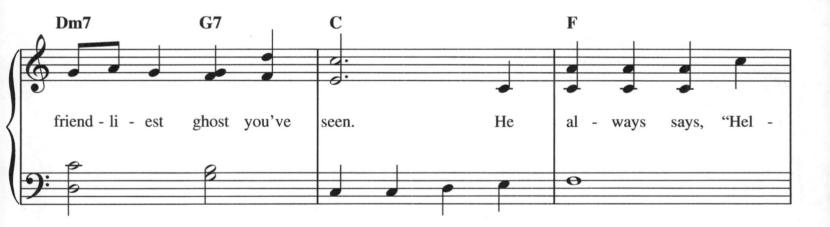

friend - li - est ghost you've seen. He al - ways says, "Hel -

lo," and he's real - ly glad to meet - cha. Wher -

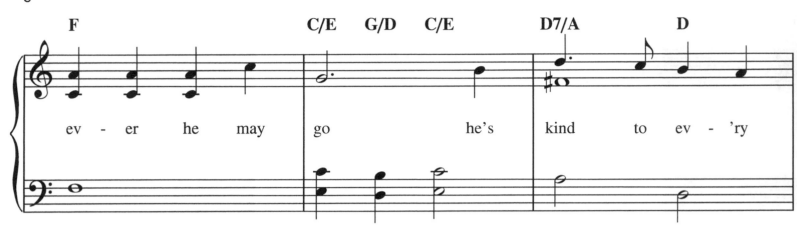

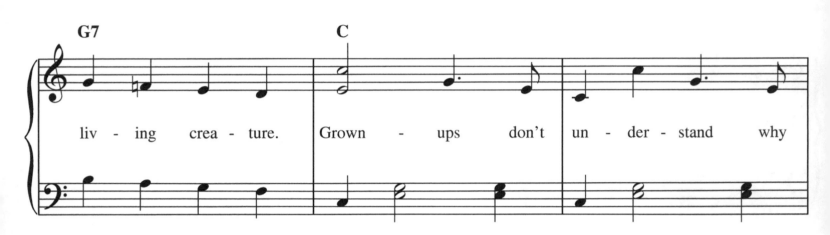

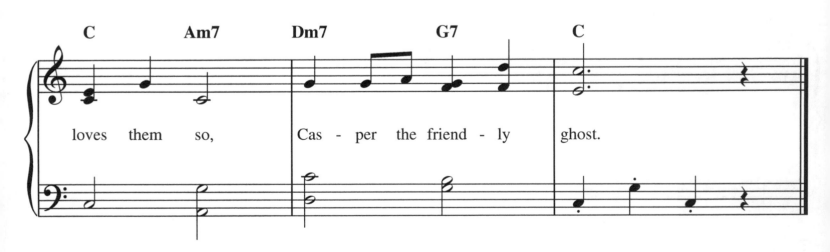

# FUNERAL MARCH
## (Piano Sonata in B-flat Minor, Op. 35)

By FREDERIC CHOPIN

# FUNERAL MARCH OF A MARIONETTE

By CHARLES GOUNOD

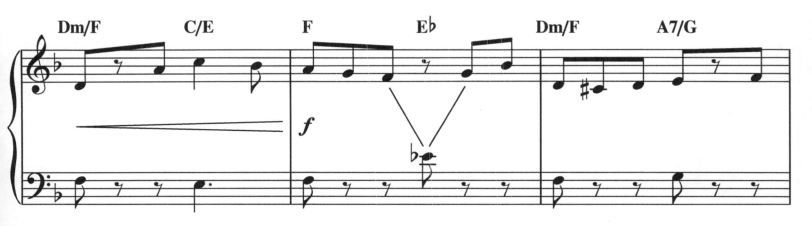

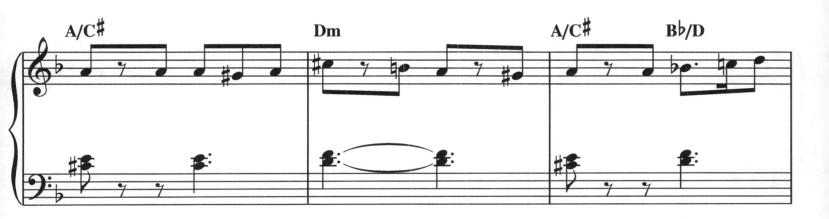

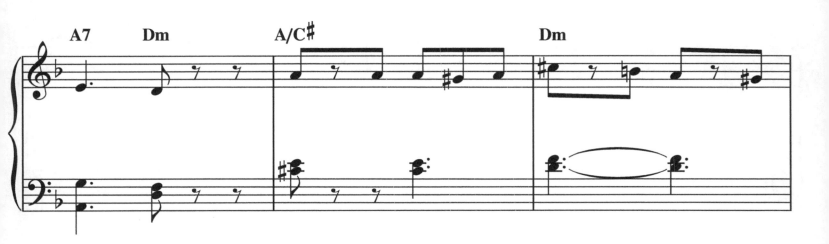

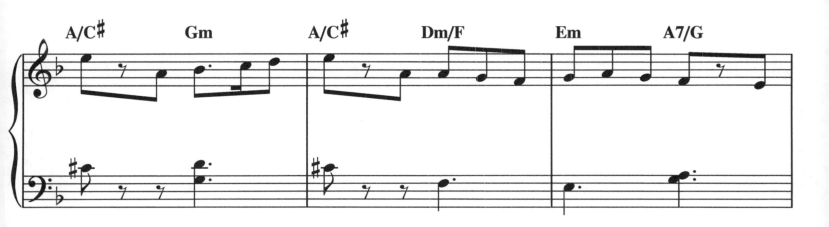

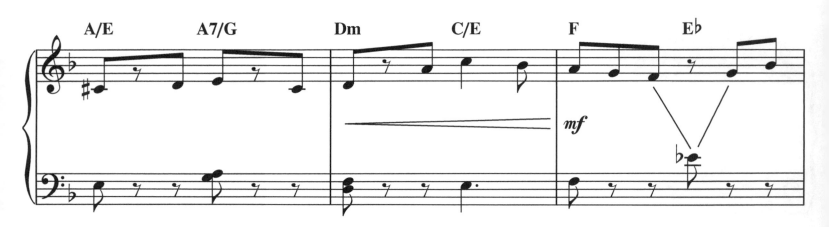

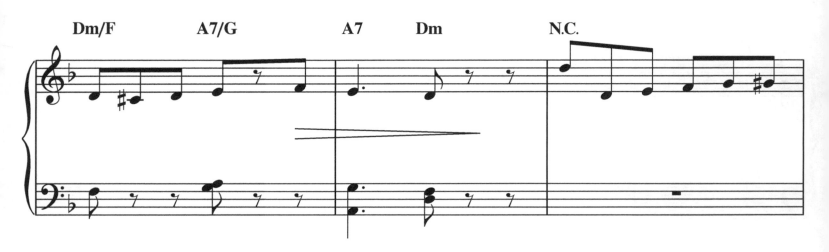

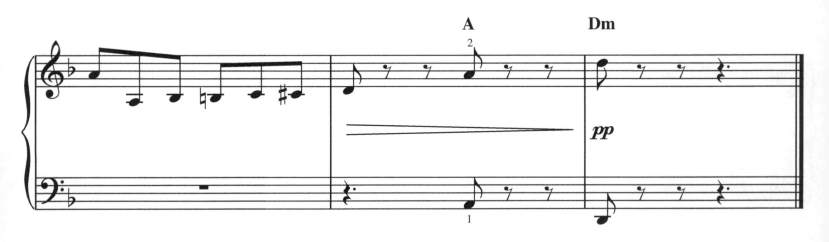

# (GHOST) RIDERS IN THE SKY
## (A Cowboy Legend)
### from RIDERS IN THE SKY

By STAN JONES

went a - long his way, _____
hot breath he could feel, _____

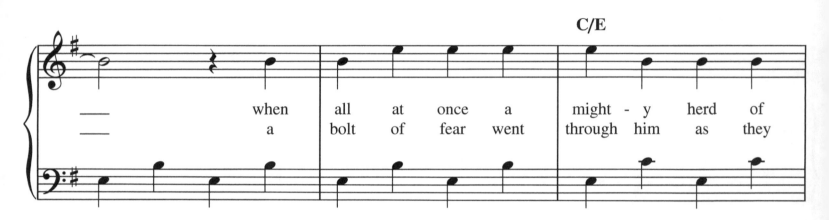

C/E

_____ when all at once a might - y herd of
_____ a bolt of fear went through him as they

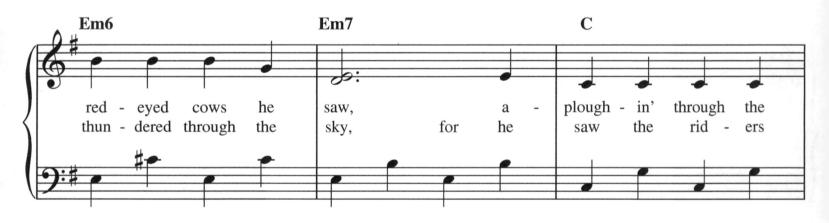

Em6                     Em7                     C

red - eyed cows he saw, a - plough - in' through the
thun - dered through the sky, for he saw the rid - ers

rag - ged skies _____ and
com - in' hard _____ and he

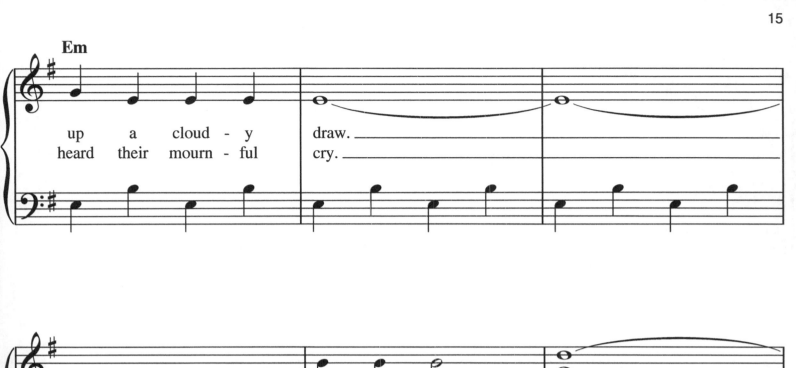

up   a   cloud - y   draw. _____

heard   their   mourn - ful   cry. _____

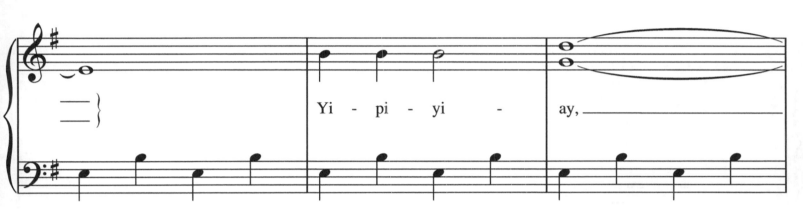

Yi - pi - yi - ay, _____

_____   Yi - pi - yi -

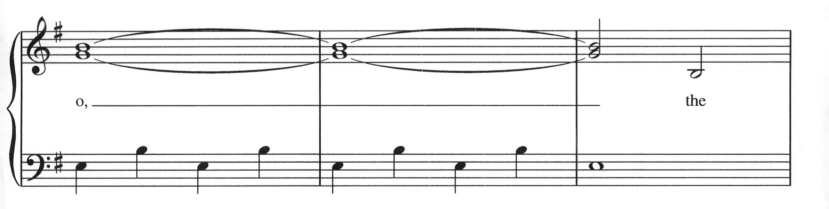

o, _____   the

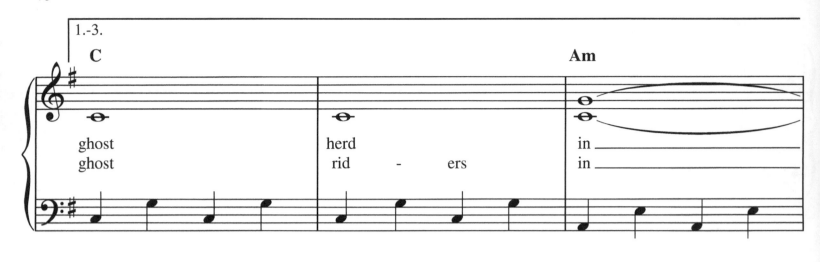

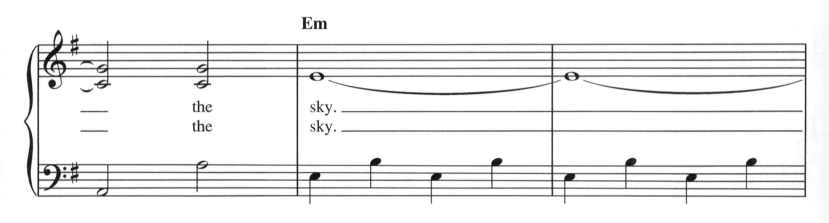

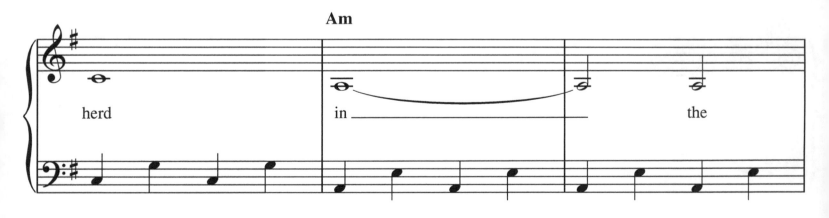

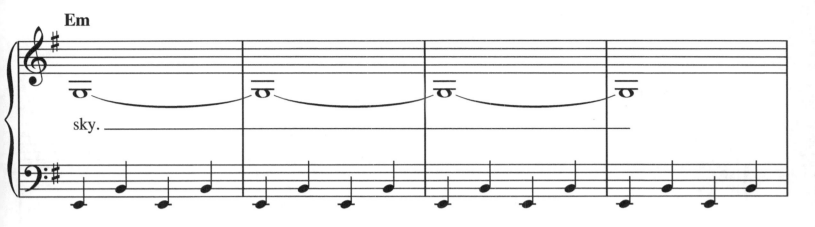

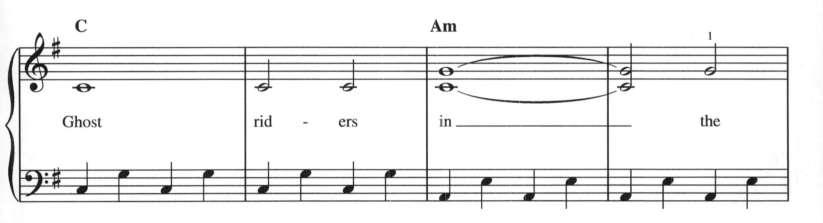

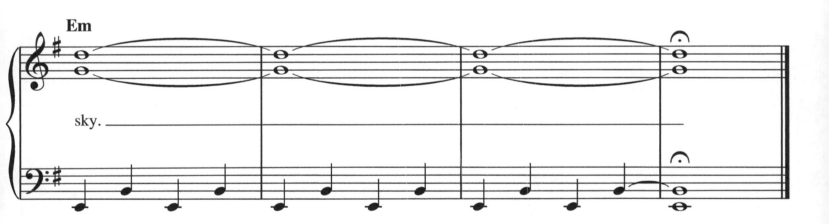

*Additional Lyrics*

3. Their faces gaunt their eyes were blurred and shirts all soaked with sweat,
They're ridin' hard to catch that herd but they ain't caught them yet,
'Cause they've got to ride forever on that range up in the sky
On horses snortin' fire as they ride on, hear their cry.
Yi-pi-yi-ay, yi-pi-yi-o, the ghost riders in the sky.

4. As the riders loped on by him he heard one call his name,
"If you want to save your soul from hell a-ridin' on our range,
Then cowboy, change your ways today or with us you will ride
A-try'n to catch the devil's herd across these endless skies."
Yi-pi-yi-ay, yi-pi-yi-o, the ghost riders in the sky. Ghost riders in the sky.

# HALLOWEEN SONG

Traditional

**Quick, but mysterious**

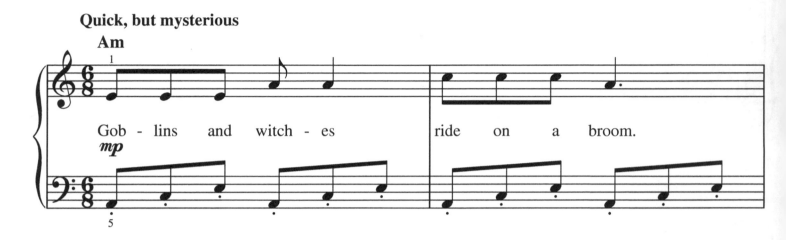

Goblins and witch - es ride on a broom.

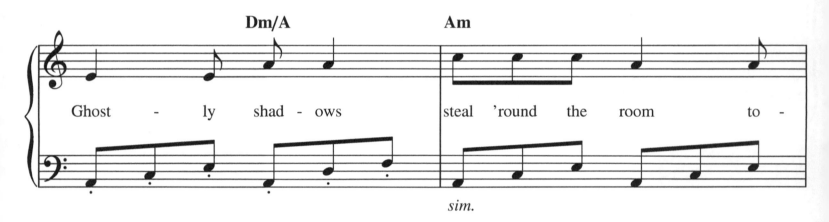

Ghost - ly shad - ows steal 'round the room to -

night. To - night is Hal - low -

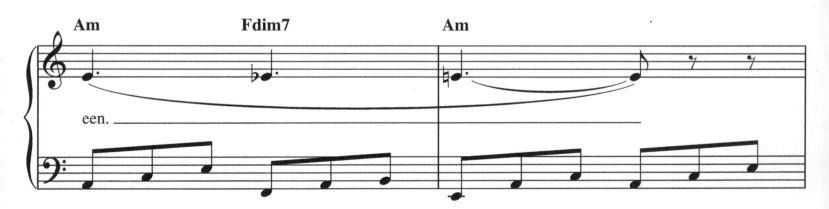

een.

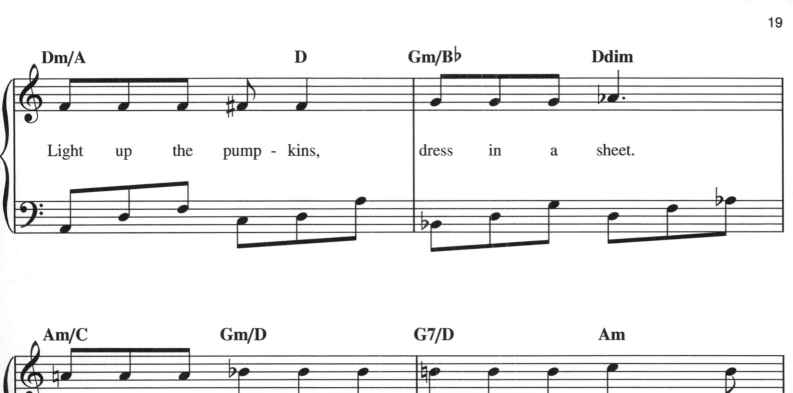

Light up the pump - kins, dress in a sheet.

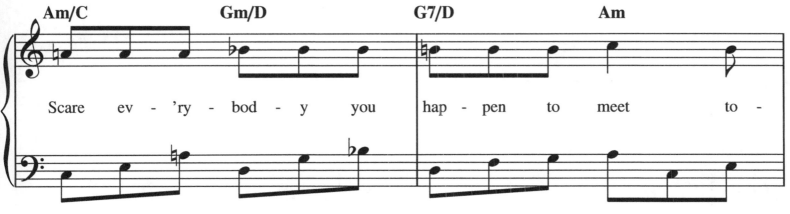

Scare ev - 'ry - bod - y you hap - pen to meet to -

night. To - night is Hal - low -

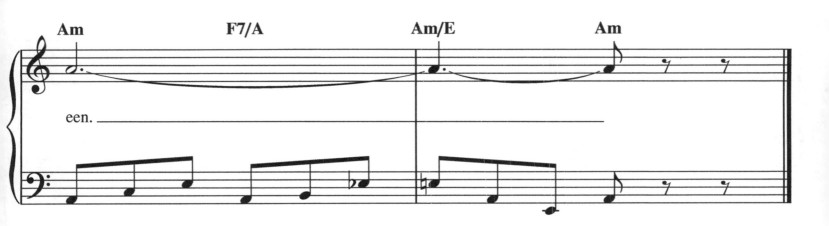

een. _____

# THEME FROM "JAWS"

**from the Universal Picture JAWS**

By JOHN WILLIAMS

**Very steady and threatening**

*8vb throughout*

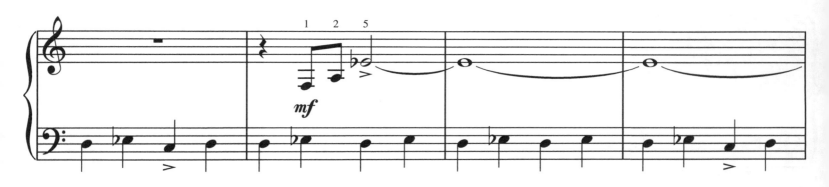

*R.H. legato*

22

**Repeat and Fade**

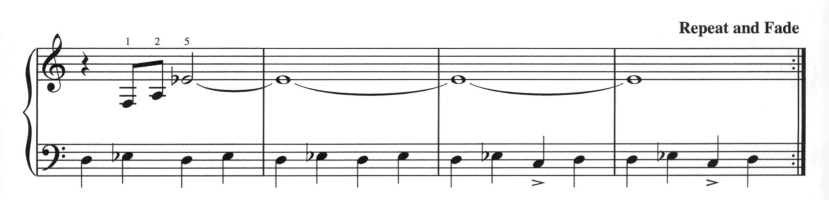

# LITTLE SHOP OF HORRORS

**from the Stage Production LITTLE SHOP OF HORRORS**

Words by HOWARD ASHMAN
Music by ALAN MENKEN

what a creep-y thing to be hap-pen-ing. Look out! Look out!

Shang-a-lang, feel the sturm and drang in the air.

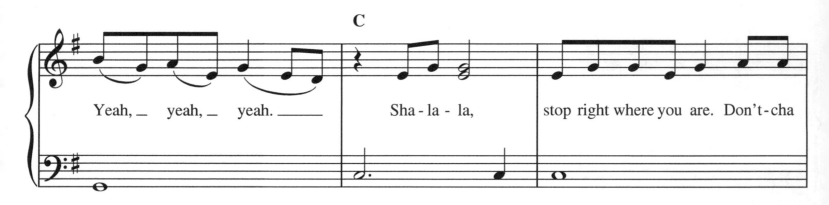

Yeah, yeah, yeah. Sha-la-la, stop right where you are. Don't-cha

move a thing. You bet-ter, you bet-ter,

tell- in' you, you bet - ter | tell your ma - ma | some-thing's gon - na get her.

**Am7**      **Am7/C**

She bet - ter,    ev-'ry-bod-y bet-ter be-ware! _____

**Am7/E**      **D7**      **D.S. al Coda**

Com-a, com-a, com-a,

**CODA**

**G**    **Am**

No,   oh,    oh,

**G/B**    **Cm**      **G/D**    **Cm/E♭**      **G**

no,    oh,    oh,    no,    oh,    oh,    no! _____

# MONSTER MASH

Words and Music by BOBBY PICKETT
and LEONARD CAPIZZI

**Medium Rock beat**

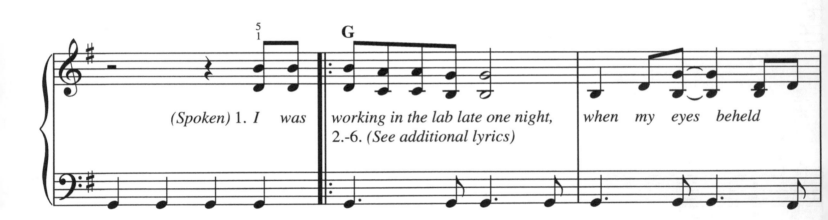

(Spoken) Mash good, easy, Igor, you impetuous

**Repeat and Fade**

young boy. Uh - uh - uh - uh.

*Additional Lyrics*

2. From my laboratory in the castle east
   To the master bedroom where the vampires feast,
   The ghouls all came from their humble abodes
   To catch a jolt from my electrodes.
   *Chorus*

3. The zombies were having fun,
   The party had just begun.
   The guests included Wolf-man,
   Dracula, and his son.
   *Chorus*

4. The scene was rockin'; all were digging the sounds,
   Igor on chains, backed by his baying hounds.
   The coffin-bangers were about to arrive
   With their vocal group, "The Crypt-Kicker Five."
   *Chorus*

5. Out from his coffin, Drac's voice did ring;
   Seems he was troubled by just one thing.
   He opened the lid and shook his fist,
   And said, "Whatever happened to my Transylvanian Twist?"
   *Chorus*

6. Now everything's cool, Drac's part of the band.
   And my monster mash is the hit of the land.
   For you, the living, this mash was meant too,
   When you get to my door, tell them Boris sent you.
   *Chorus*

# THE MUNSTERS THEME

**from the Television Series**

By JACK MARSHALL

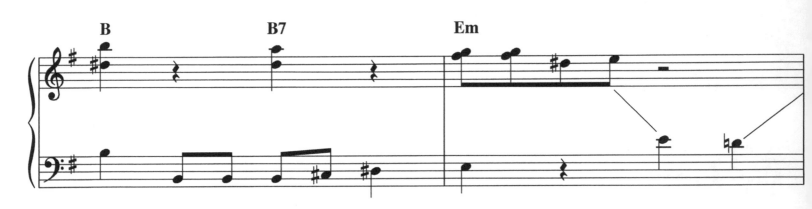

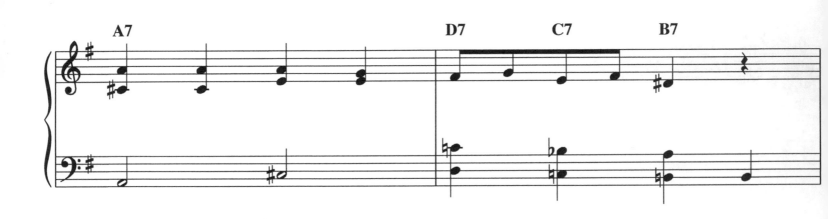

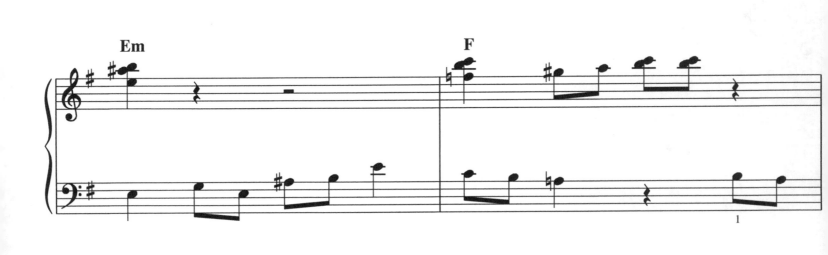

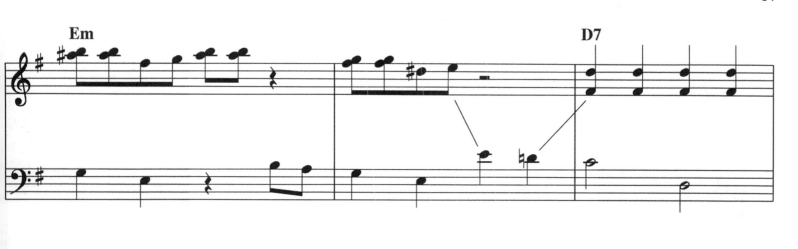

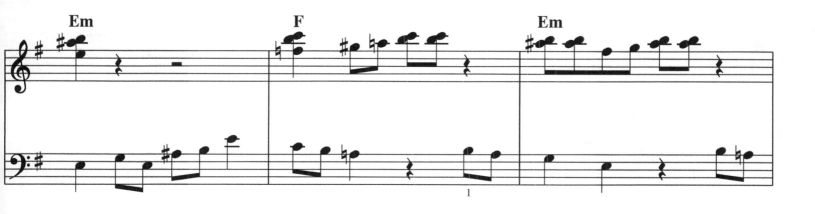

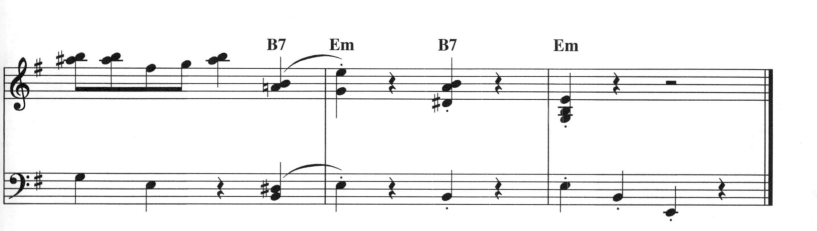

# (IT'S A) MONSTER'S HOLIDAY

Words and Music by
BUCK OWENS

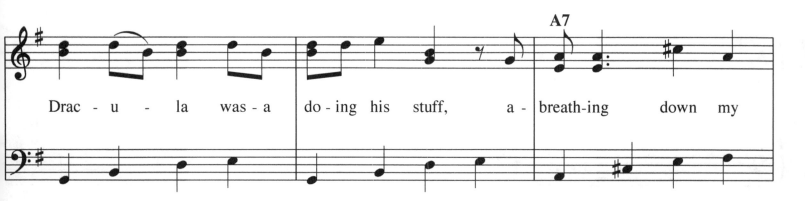

Drac - u - la was - a do - ing his stuff, a - breath-ing down my

neck. Jump back,— make tracks, here comes the Hunch - back,

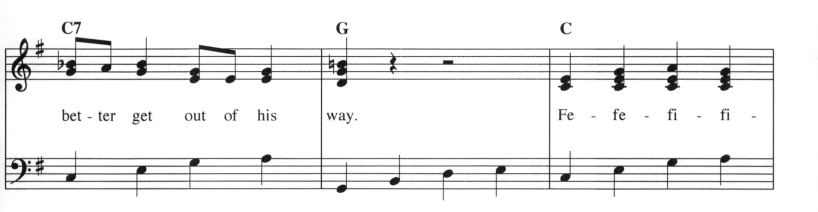

bet - ter get out of his way. Fe - fe - fi - fi -

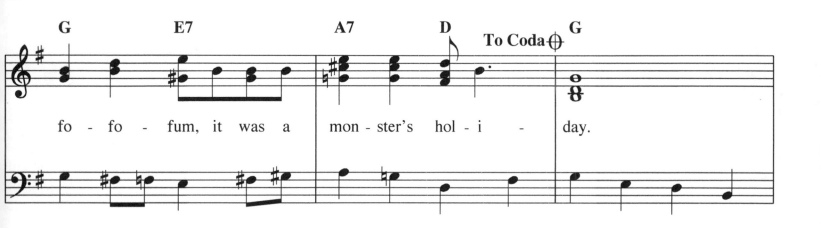

fo - fo - fum, it was a mon - ster's hol - i - day.

Well, I hopped in-to bed and I cov-ered up my head, _ said,"I'm
Un - cle __ Bill, well, _ he took _____ ill ___ and they

**C7**

gon - na get a good night's sleep." I got woke up a-bout
sent for _____ me to come. Well, I had to pass by

**A7**         **D7**

twelve o' - clock _ and I jumped right to my feet. There was
the old grave yard ___ so I went on the run. There was

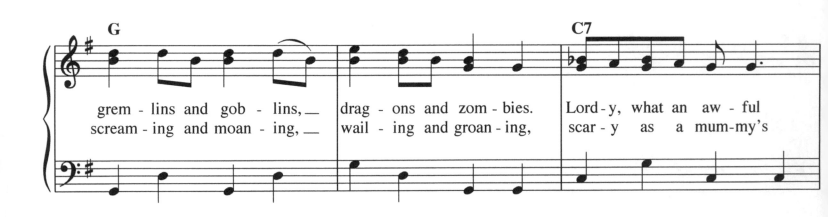

**G**         **C7**

grem - lins and gob - lins, __ drag - ons and zom - bies. Lord - y, what an aw - ful
scream - ing and moan - ing, __ wail - ing and groan - ing, scar - y as a mum-my's

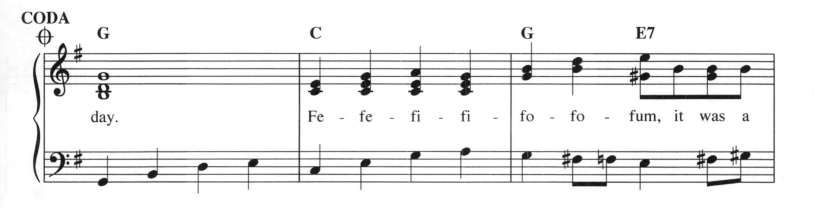

# PURPLE PEOPLE EATER

Words and Music by
SHEB WOOLEY

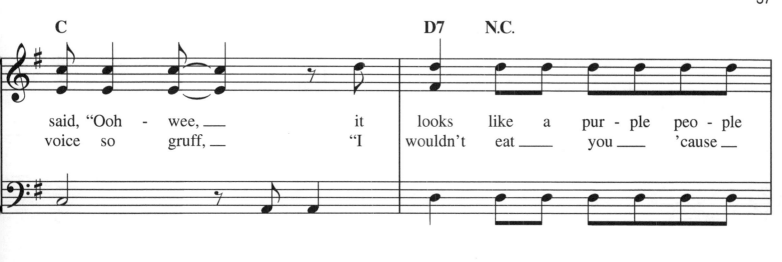

said, "Ooh - wee, ___ it looks like a pur - ple peo - ple
voice so gruff, ___ "I wouldn't eat ___ you ___ 'cause ___

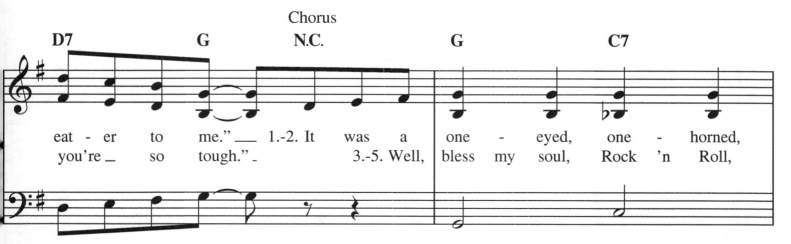

Chorus

eat - er to me." ___ 1.-2. It was a one - eyed, one - horned,
you're ___ so tough." ___ 3.-5. Well, bless my soul, Rock 'n Roll,

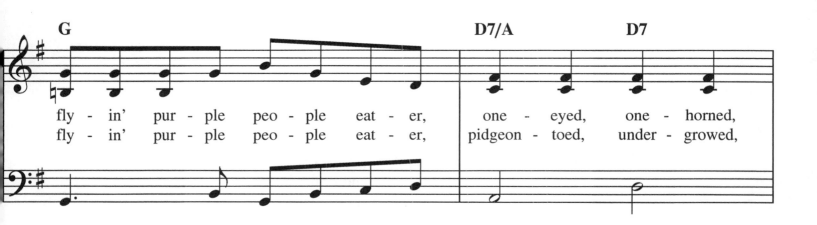

fly - in' pur - ple peo - ple eat - er, one - eyed, one - horned,
fly - in' pur - ple peo - ple eat - er, pidgeon - toed, under - growed,

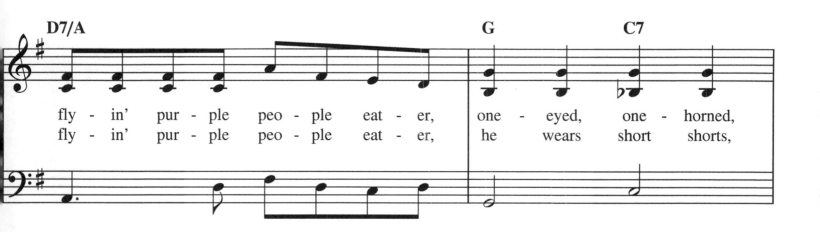

fly - in' pur - ple peo - ple eat - er, one - eyed, one - horned,
fly - in' pur - ple peo - ple eat - er, he wears short shorts,

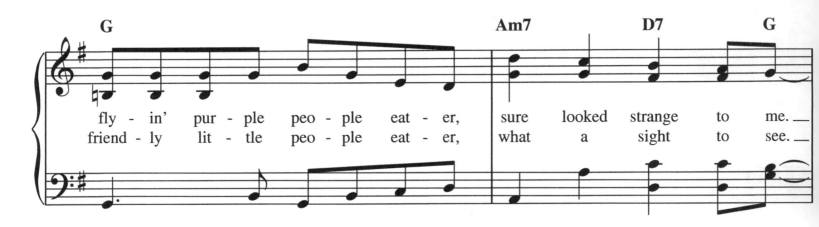

fly - in' pur - ple peo - ple eat - er, sure looked strange to me. ___
friend - ly lit - tle peo - ple eat - er, what a sight to see. ___

2. Well, he

*Additional Lyrics*

3. I said, "Mister purple people eater, what's your line?"
   He said, "Eatin' purple people, and it sure is fine,
   But that's not the reason that I came to land,
   I wanna get a job in a rock and roll band."
   *Chorus*

4. And then he swung from the tree and he lit on the ground,
   And he started to rock, a-really rockin' around.
   It was a crazy ditty with a swingin' tune,
   Singa bop bapa loop a lap a loom bam boom.
   *Chorus*

5. Well, he went on his way and then what-a you know,
   I saw him last night on a T.V. show.
   He was blowin' it out, really knockin' 'em dead.
   Playin' rock 'n roll music through the horn of his head.
   *Chorus*

# SONG OF THE VOLGA BOATMAN

Russian Folk Song

# THE SORCERER'S APPRENTICE

### from FANTASIA

By PAUL DUKAS

**Moderately fast**

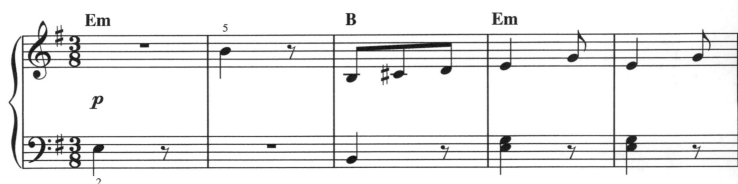

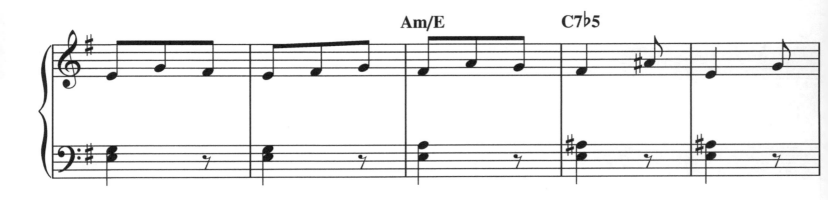

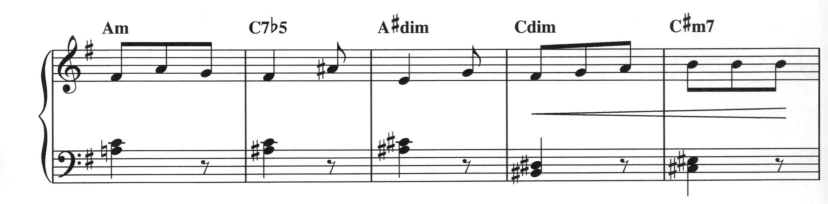

# THE THING

Words and Music by
CHARLES R. GREAN

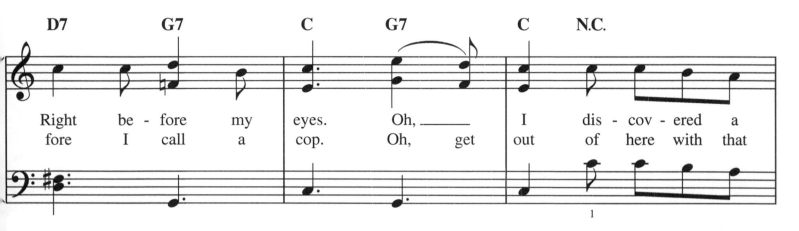

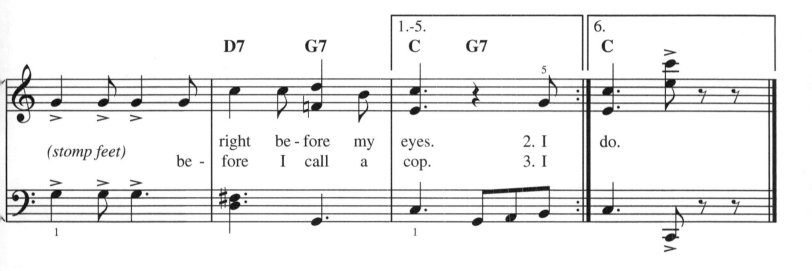

*Additional Lyrics*

3. I turned and got right out a-runnin' for my life,
   And then I took it home with me to give it to my wife.
   But this is what she hollered at me as I walked in the door:
   Oh, get out of here with that (xxx) and don't come back no more.
   Oh, get out of here with that (xxx) and don't come back no more.

4. I wandered all around the town until I chanced to meet
   A hobo who was looking for a handout on the street.
   He said he'd take most any old thing, he was a desperate man,
   But when I showed him the (xxx), he turned around and ran.
   Oh, when I showed him the (xxx), he turned around and ran.

5. I wandered on for many years, a victim of my fate,
   Until one day I came upon Saint Peter at the gate.
   And when I tried to take it inside he told me where to go:
   Get out of here with that (xxx) and take it down below.
   Oh, get out of here with that (xxx) and take it down below.

6. The moral of the story is if you're out on the beach
   And you should see a great big box and it's within your reach,
   Don't ever stop and open it up, that's my advice to you,
   'Cause you'll never get rid of the (xxx), no matter what you do.
   Oh, you'll never get rid of the (xxx), no matter what you do.

# THIS IS HALLOWEEN

from Tim Burton's THE NIGHTMARE BEFORE CHRISTMAS

Music and Lyrics by
DANNY ELFMAN

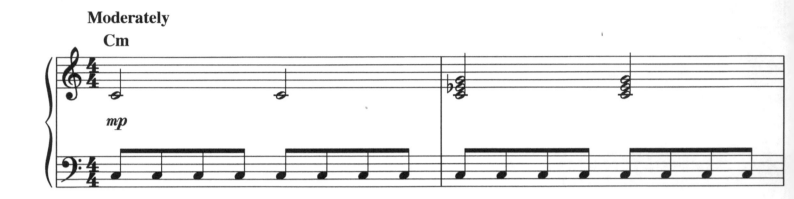

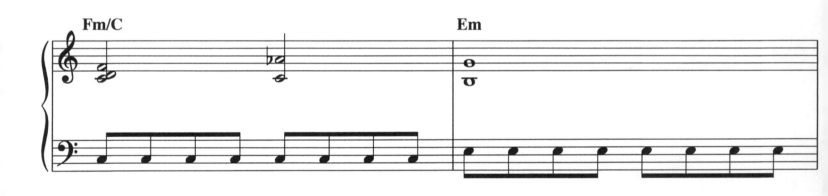

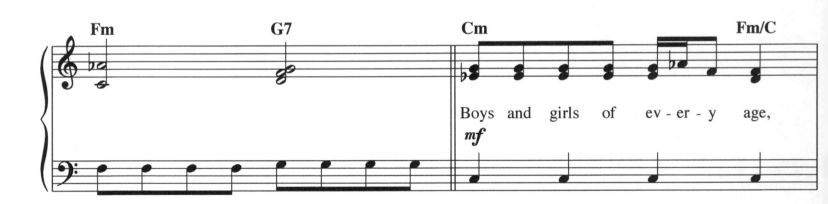

Boys and girls of ev-er-y age,

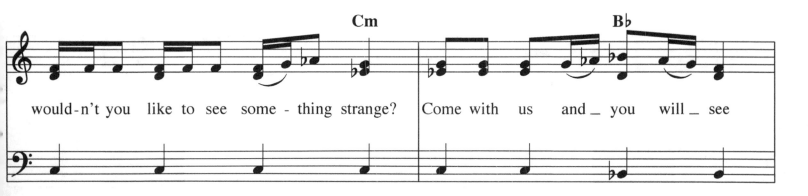

would-n't you like to see some - thing strange? Come with us and _ you will _ see

this, our town _ of Hal - low - een! __ This is Hal-low-een, this is Hal-low-een!

Pump-kins scream in the dead of night! This is Hal-low-een, ev-'ry-bod-y make a scene.

*(Spoken:)*
Trick or treat *'til the neigh-bors gon-na die of fright.* It's our town. Ev-'ry-bod-y scream_

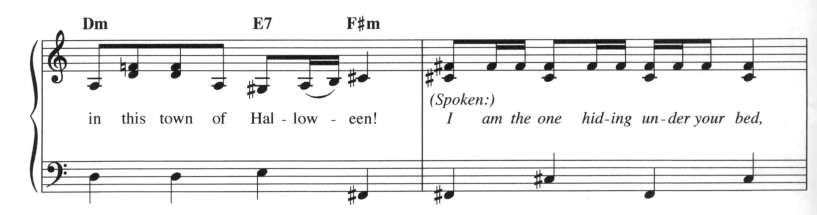

in this town of Hal - low - een!

(Spoken:)
I am the one hid-ing un-der your bed,

teeth ground sharp and eyes glow-ing red!

I am the one hid-ing un-der your stairs,

fin-gers like snakes and spi-ders in my hair!

This is Hal-low-een, this is Hal-low-een,

Hal-low-een! Hal-low-een! Hal-low-een! Hal-low-een!

# It's Easy to Play Your Favorite Songs with Hal Leonard Easy Piano Books

### The Best Praise & Worship Songs Ever

The name says it all: over 70 of the best P&W songs today. Titles include: Awesome God • Blessed Be Your Name • Come, Now Is the Time to Worship • Days of Elijah • Here I Am to Worship • Open the Eyes of My Heart • Shout to the Lord • We Fall Down • and more.
00311312 ..................... $19.99

### First 50 Popular Songs You Should Play on the Piano

50 great pop classics for beginning pianists to learn, including: Candle in the Wind • Chopsticks • Don't Know Why • Hallelujah • Happy Birthday to You • Heart and Soul • I Walk the Line • Just the Way You Are • Let It Be • Let It Go • Over the Rainbow • Piano Man • and many more.
00131140 .......................... $16.99

### The Greatest Video Game Music

28 easy piano selections for the music that envelops you as you lose yourself in the world of video games, including: Angry Birds Theme • Assassin's Creed Revelations • Dragonborn (Skyrim Theme) • Elder Scrolls: Oblivion • Minecraft: Sweden • Rage of Sparta from God of War III • and more.
00202545 ...................... $17.99

### Jumbo Easy Piano Songbook

200 classical favorites, folk songs and jazz standards. Includes: Amazing Grace • Beale Street Blues • Bridal Chorus • Buffalo Gals • Canon in D • Cielito Lindo • Danny Boy • The Entertainer • Für Elise • Greensleeves • Jamaica Farewell • Marianne • Molly Malone • Ode to Joy • Peg O' My Heart • Rockin' Robin • Yankee Doodle • dozens more!
00311014 ........................... $19.99

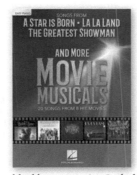

### Songs from *A Star Is Born, The Greatest Showman, La La Land*, and More Movie Musicals

Movie musical lovers will delight in this songbook chock full of top-notch songs arranged for easy piano with lyrics from blockbuster movies. Includes: City of Stars from *La La Land* • Suddenly from *Les Misérables* • This Is Me from *The Greatest Showman* • Shallow from *A Star Is Born* • and more.
00287577 ............................. $17.99

### 50 Easy Classical Themes

Easy arrangements of 50 classical tunes representing more than 30 composers, including: Bach, Beethoven, Chopin, Debussy, Dvorak, Handel, Haydn, Liszt, Mozart, Mussorgsky, Puccini, Rossini, Schubert, Strauss, Tchaikovsky, Vivaldi, and more.
00311215 ................................. $14.99

### Pop Songs for Kids

Kids from all corners of the world love and sing along to the songs of Taylor Swift, One Direction, Katy Perry, and other pop stars. This collection features 25 songs from these and many more artists in easy piano format. Includes: Brave • Can't Stop the Feeling • Firework • Home • Let It Go • Shake It Off • What Makes You Beautiful • and more.
00221920 ......................... $14.99

### Simple Songs – The Easiest Easy Piano Songs

Play 50 of your favorite songs in the easiest of arrangements! Songs include: Castle on a Cloud • Do-Re-Mi • Happy Birthday to You • Hey Jude • Let It Go • Linus and Lucy • Over the Rainbow • Smile • Star Wars (Main Theme) • Tomorrow • and more.
00142041 .......................... $14.99

### VH1's 100 Greatest Songs of Rock and Roll

The results from the VH1 show that featured the 100 greatest rock and roll songs of all time are here in this awesome collection! Songs include: Born to Run • Good Vibrations • Hey Jude • Hotel California • Imagine • Light My Fire • Like a Rolling Stone • Respect • and more.
00311110 ..............................$29.99

### River Flows in You and Other Eloquent Songs for Easy Piano Solo

24 piano favorites arranged so that even beginning players can sound great. Includes: All of Me • Bella's Lullaby • Cristofori's Dream • Il Postino (The Postman) • Jessica's Theme (Breaking in the Colt) • The John Dunbar Theme • and more.
00137581 .............................$14.99

### Disney's My First Song Book

16 favorite songs to sing and play. Every page is beautifully illustrated with full-color art from Disney features. Songs include: Beauty and the Beast • Bibbidi-Bobbidi-Boo • Circle of Life • Cruella De Vil • A Dream Is a Wish Your Heart Makes • Hakuna Matata • Under the Sea • Winnie the Pooh • You've Got a Friend in Me • and more.
00310322 ..............................$17.99

### Top Hits of 2019

20 of the year's best are included in this collection arranged for easy piano with lyrics. Includes: Bad Guy (Billie Eilish) • I Don't Care (Ed Sheeran & Justin Bieber) • ME! (Taylor Swift feat. Brendon Urie) • Old Town Road (Remix) (Lil Nas X feat. Billy Ray Cyrus) • Senorita (Shawn Mendes & Camila Cabello) • Someone You Loved (Lewis Capaldi) • and more.
00302273 ..................................$16.99

Get complete song lists and more at
**www.halleonard.com**

*Pricess, contents, and availability subject to change without notice*
*Disney characters and artwork © Disney Enterprises, Inc.*

# POP PIANO HITS

*Pop Piano Hits is a series designed for students of all ages. Each book contains five simple and easy-to-read arrangements of today's most popular downloads. Lyrics, fingering and chord symbols are included to help you make the most of each arrangement. Enjoy your favorite songs and artists today!*

### BELIEVER, WHAT ABOUT US & MORE HOT SINGLES
Attention (Charlie Puth) • Believer (Imagine Dragons) • There's Nothing Holdin' Me Back (Shawn Mendes) • Too Good at Goodbyes (Sam Smith) • What About Us (P!nk).
00251934 Easy Piano . . . . . . . . . . . . . . . . . . $9.99

### BLANK SPACE, I REALLY LIKE YOU & MORE HOT SINGLES
Blank Space (Taylor Swift) • Heartbeat Song (Kelly Clarkson) • I Really Like You (Carly Rae Jepsen) • I'm Not the Only One (Sam Smith) • Thinking Out Loud (Ed Sheeran).
00146286 Easy Piano . . . . . . . . . . . . . . . . . . $9.99

### CAN'T STOP THE FEELING, 7 YEARS & MORE HOT SINGLES
Can't Stop the Feeling (Justin Timberlake) • H.O.L.Y. (Florida Georgia Line) • Just Like Fire (Pink) • Lost Boy (Ruth B.) • 7 Years (Lukas Graham).
00193755 Easy Piano . . . . . . . . . . . . . . . . . . $9.99

### CITY OF STARS, MERCY & MORE HOT SINGLES
City of Stars (from *La La Land*) • Evermore (from *Beauty and the Beast*) • Mercy (Shawn Mendes) • Perfect (Ed Sheeran) • Stay (Zedd & Alessia Cara).
00236097 Easy Piano . . . . . . . . . . . . . . . . . . $9.99

### FEEL IT STILL, REWRITE THE STARS & MORE HOT SINGLES
Feel It Still (Portugal. The Man) • Lost in Japan (Shawn Mendes) • The Middle (Zedd, Maren Morris & Grey) • Rewrite the Stars (from *The Greatest Showman*) • Whatever It Takes (Imagine Dragons).
00278090 Easy Piano . . . . . . . . . . . . . . . . . . $9.99

### GIRLS LIKE YOU, HAPPY NOW & MORE HOT SINGLES
Girls Like You (Maroon 5) • Happy Now (Zedd feat. Elley Duhé) • Treat Myself (Meghan Trainor) • You Are the Reason (Calum Scott) • You Say (Lauren Daigle).
00285014 Easy Piano . . . . . . . . . . . . . . . . . . $9.99

### HOW FAR I'LL GO, THIS TOWN & MORE HOT SINGLES
How Far I'll Go (Alessia Cara - from *Moana*) • My Way (Calvin Harris) • This Town (Niall Horan) • Treat You Better (Shawn Mendes) • We Don't Talk Anymore (Charlie Puth feat. Selena Gomez).
00211286 Easy Piano . . . . . . . . . . . . . . . . . . $9.99

### LET IT GO, HAPPY & MORE HOT SINGLES
All of Me (John Legend) • Dark Horse (Katy Perry) • Happy (Pharrell) • Let It Go (Demi Lovato) • Pompeii (Bastille).
00128204 Easy Piano . . . . . . . . . . . . . . . . . . $9.99

### LOVE YOURSELF, STITCHES & MORE HOT SINGLES
Like I'm Gonna Lose You (Meghan Trainor) • Love Yourself (Justin Bieber) • One Call Away (Charlie Puth) • Stitches (Shawn Mendes) • Stressed Out (Twenty One Pilots).
00159285 Easy Piano . . . . . . . . . . . . . . . . . . $9.99

### ROAR, ROYALS & MORE HOT SINGLES
Atlas (Coldplay – from *The Hunger Games: Catching Fire*) • Roar (Katy Perry) • Royals (Lorde) • Safe and Sound (Capital Cities) • Wake Me Up! (Avicii).
00123868 Easy Piano . . . . . . . . . . . . . . . . . . $9.99

### SAY SOMETHING, COUNTING STARS & MORE HOT SINGLES
Counting Stars (One Republic) • Demons (Imagine Dragons) • Let Her Go (Passenger) • Say Something (A Great Big World) • Story of My Life (One Direction).
00125356 Easy Piano . . . . . . . . . . . . . . . . . . $9.99

### SEE YOU AGAIN, FLASHLIGHT & MORE HOT SINGLES
Budapest (George Ezra) • Flashlight (Jessie J.) • Honey I'm Good (Andy Grammer) • See You Again (Wiz Khalifa) • Shut Up and Dance (Walk the Moon).
00150045 Easy Piano . . . . . . . . . . . . . . . . . . $9.99

### SHAKE IT OFF, ALL ABOUT THAT BASS & MORE HOT SINGLES
All About That Bass (Meghan Trainor) • Shake It Off (Taylor Swift) • A Sky Full of Stars (Coldplay) • Something in the Water (Carrie Underwood) • Take Me to Church (Hozier).
00142734 Easy Piano . . . . . . . . . . . . . . . . . . $9.99

### SUNFLOWER, WITHOUT ME & MORE HOT SINGLES
High Hopes (Panic! at the Disco) • No Place (Backstreet Boys) • Shallow (Lady Gaga and Bradley Cooper) • Sunflower (Post Malone) • Without Me (Halsey).
00291634 Easy Piano . . . . . . . . . . . . . . . . . . $9.99

**HAL•LEONARD®**

**www.halleonard.com**